BEFORE I MADE HISTORY™

Let's Ride, Paul Revere!

by Peter and Connie Roop

10650729

SCHOLASTIC INC.

New York   Toronto   London   Auckland   Sydney
Mexico City   New Delhi   Hong Kong   Buenos Aires

For Leah and Richard

"Listen, my friends, and you shall hear
Marvelous stories, both far and near."

The authors would like to thank Patrick Leehey
of the Paul Revere House in Boston for his
cheerful, expert assistance!

ISBN 0-439-67623-1

12 11 10 9 8 7 6 5 4 3 2 1   4 5 6 7 8 9/0

Printed in the U.S.A.   40
First printing, September 2004

Table of Contents

Introduction

Paul Revere is famous for his ride on the night of April 18, 1775. That night, Paul Revere galloped across the Massachusetts countryside to warn American Patriots that British soldiers were coming. The soldiers hoped to capture American cannons, guns, and gunpowder in Concord.

Paul also warned John Hancock and Sam Adams. These two Patriot leaders were in Lexington, Massachusetts. Paul told them that the British would be coming to arrest them.

In 1861, Henry Wadsworth Longfellow published his popular poem "Paul Revere's Ride." Paul Revere became an American hero. His poem begins with these lines:

1

Listen, my children, and you shall hear
Of the midnight ride of Paul Revere.

Longfellow's poem made Paul Revere famous. Do you know that there are towns in Massachusetts, Missouri, and Minnesota named Revere?

As a silversmith, Paul Revere made spoons, bowls, teapots, and ladles. Do you know Paul also made bells and cannons?

Paul Revere enjoyed Boston's many church bells. Do you know Paul was a bell ringer when he was a teenager?

Paul Revere warned American Patriots that the British were coming. Do you know other riders rode that same night giving the same warning?

The answers to these questions and many more lie in who Paul Revere was as a boy and as a young man. This book is about Paul Revere before he made history.

1
Paul Revere Is Born

Tuesday, December 21, 1734, was a cold day in Boston, Massachusetts Bay Colony. But inside the Revere house, it was warm. Deborah Revere held their son as Master Paul Revere proudly smiled. The new baby was named after his father, Paul. The Reveres' first child, Deborah, had been born two years earlier, in 1732. She was named after her mother.

Paul Revere was gently carried to Cockerel Church. Friends and family joined Paul's father as Reverend Welsteed baptized Paul. Paul's mother was home resting. Before long, Paul was back in her arms. Friends crowded into the Revere home to celebrate Paul's birth.

Paul's father was a silversmith. He made silver spoons, buckles, teapots, dishes, cups, and bowls. He had his own silver shop in Boston. Paul's father proudly stamped P. RE-VERE on his silver.

Paul's mother was named Deborah Hitchbourn Revere. Her father owned Hitchbourn's Wharf. Hitchbourn's Wharf stretched into Boston Bay. It wasn't the longest wharf in Boston, but it was one of the busiest.

Boston was the busiest seaport in the thirteen colonies. Hundreds of ships, mostly British, sailed to Boston every year. The ships brought books, paper, glass, tea, pottery, china, silk, lace, molasses, tools, and spices. The ships left loaded with lumber and fish.

Hustling, bustling Boston was almost surrounded by water. This helped Boston become a valuable seaport. But it meant Boston's 15,000 people were crowded into a small space.

Boston Neck, a narrow strip of land, connected Boston to the mainland. A gate at Boston Neck guarded the entrance into the city by land. When the tide was especially high, Boston Neck was covered with water and Boston became an island.

Boston was a town of bells. Chiming church bells called people to worship. Clanging bells warned of fires. Schoolmasters shook handheld bells. Bells tolled when someone died. Pealing bells announced the opening of the markets. Cowbells jingled. Peddlers' bells jangled.

Boston was a lively, noisy town in 1734 when Paul Revere was born. Carriages and wagons rolled along crooked cobblestone streets like Love Lane, Fish Street, and Ship Street. Merchants and shopkeepers had colorful signs swinging outside their shops.

Farmers sold meat, fruit, and vegetables in markets. Fishermen, tooting tin whistles, peddled fresh cod, salmon, and mackerel. Boys shouting "Lobs! Lobs! Lobs!" sold live lobsters. Sailors and sea captains strolled the streets. Apprentices ran errands. Students played on their way to school.

Hungry pigs wandered the streets. Cows

grazed on Boston Common, a public field. Dogs chased cats. Cats chased rats and mice. Seagulls soared.

Blacksmiths forged horseshoes, tools, and wheels. Carpenters hammered wood. Candlemakers molded candles and shaped soap. Shipwrights built ships. Sailmakers sewed sails. Rope makers twisted miles of rope. Silversmiths like Paul's father fashioned silver spoons, teapots, sugar bowls, buttons, buckles, and dishes.

Boston was Paul's world. Paul loved Boston so much that one day he would risk his life for the town.

2

Paul Revere's Early Years

No one knows exactly where Paul Revere's first home was. Most likely it was on North Street, near Love Lane in the center of Boston's North End. Like most Boston homes, Paul's house was probably made of wood. It stood two or three stories tall.

Paul's father made a good living as a silversmith. His father wasn't rich, but he provided well for his growing family. Paul Revere had eleven brothers and sisters.

Paul's father's silver shop was probably on the first floor of the Revere home. Paul grew up listening to the tap of his father's hammers. Paul smelled charcoal burning in the furnace to melt silver. He heard customers placing orders.

Paul spent most of his time in the main room on the first floor. This large room was the kitchen, dining room, laundry, family room, and sometimes the bedroom.

A tall fireplace warmed the first floor. Here, Deborah Revere cooked her family's meals. She roasted chickens and turkeys. She baked beans and puddings. She cooked fish and chowders. As a young boy, Paul watched his mother and sisters cook, sew, wash clothes, and preserve food. When he was older, Paul carried wood and water.

Paul didn't have his own bedroom. He slept in the attic with his brothers. Like most Boston families, the Reveres kept chickens. The chickens provided eggs for eating and baking. The Reveres probably had a pig and a cow, too.

Paul played with his brothers, his sisters, and his many Hitchbourn cousins. The Hitchbourns and the Reveres lived in the same neighborhood. Young Paul liked to visit his mother's aunt. Paul enjoyed her stories about Native Americans, her family, and growing up in early colonial days.

On hot summer days, Paul dived off a wharf to swim in the ocean. Years later, Paul drew a picture of a fort in Boston Harbor with three boys swimming in the water.

Paul was careful. Broken barrels, dead fish, tree stumps, and garbage floated by the wharves. Large and small boats sailed close to the wharves, too. One relative drowned after falling off a wharf. A friend almost drowned, too. On winter days, Paul and his friends sledded on Beacon Hill, skated on Frog Pond, and had snowball fights.

The Reveres went to Cockerel Church on Sunday, their day of rest. Deborah Revere didn't cook on Sundays. She prepared a pot of beans on Saturday. She placed the pot by the fire to bake all night. On Sunday, the Reveres ate delicious Boston baked beans.

Paul went to an infant school when he was about five. Infant schools were taught by women in their own homes. Paul practiced his ABC's and learned some writing and reading.

3
Paul Revere Goes to School

When he was about seven years old, Paul went to North Writing School. The Reveres helped pay for firewood to warm the school. North Writing School had two stories. Paul learned writing on the first floor. He studied reading on the second floor.

Master Zachariah Hicks was Paul's school-master. Master Hicks made sure Paul paid attention. He listened to Paul recite his reading lessons. Paul probably read the popular *New England Primer*, with verses like "My Book and Heart Shall Never Part."

Master Hicks taught Paul how to write cursive. Paul practiced until his handwriting was excellent. Paul wrote with a quill pen and homemade ink. When he was old

enough, Paul carried his own penknife to sharpen his quill pen. All his life, Paul signed his name in bold, flowing, easy-to-read letters.

Paul enjoyed reading. He read newspapers, books, and pamphlets. When he was older, Paul read chemistry books to learn how to make better copper. Once, Paul found a mistake in a chemistry book. He wrote to the author and politely pointed out the error. Paul also enjoyed writing letters to friends in the colonies and his relatives in Europe.

Paul went to school every day except Sunday. He had no summer vacation, but he did have special holidays. Election Day, when local officials were chosen, was one such holiday. Another special holiday was Training Day. On this day, Paul watched the colonial soldiers train on Boston Common.

Johnny Tileston, one of Paul's schoolmates, grew up to be the master of North Writing School. Johnny was a popular teacher. Love Lane, where Paul's school stood, was changed to Tileston Street to honor Master Tileston. Today, you can walk along Tileston Street in Paul's old neighborhood.

Paul probably learned math from his father. Paul helped his father keep the account books in the silversmith shop. Knowing math was important for a silversmith. He had to weigh every piece of silver. Even the tiny scraps on the floor were swept up and weighed. Paul's father sometimes paid for things with these scraps. He might make a dish or a spoon when he had enough scraps of silver.

When Paul was young, there weren't many banks. People had silversmiths make their silver coins into ladles, teapots, spoons, and tankards, a kind of drinking mug. When people needed money, they had their candlesticks melted and they sold the silver. Paul's father might make a beautiful bowl one day, only to melt it again when its owner needed money.

In 1743, the Reveres moved. Paul was nine years old. Paul's parents rented a shop and house from Dr. John Clark. Paul's new home was on Fish Street at the head of Dr. Clark's Wharf. Clark's Wharf was the second most important wharf in Boston. Only Long Wharf, two thousand feet long, was more important.

Dr. Clark's Wharf was a perfect place for the Revere silver shop. Wealthy merchants and ship owners did business on the wharf. They bought silver pitchers, teapots, bowls, and spoons. Sea captains spent their money on silver presents for their wives and sweethearts.

When Paul walked onto the wharf, he saw Boston's many islands. Noodle's Island looked like a polar bear. Governor's Island was shaped like a ham.

Paul could also see the cannons at the British fort on Castle Island. One day, patriotic Paul Revere would be in charge of those Castle Island cannons. Paul would use them to fight the British.

4
Paul Revere, Apprentice

Paul left North Writing School when he was about thirteen. Paul's father wanted him to become his apprentice. In return, he would provide Paul with food, lodging, and clothing.

Like all beginning apprentices, Paul did the jobs that no one else wanted to do. He carried charcoal to the furnace. He pumped the heavy bellows to keep the charcoal burning-hot. He swept sand off the floor and sifted it to save silver and gold scraps. He carried water and ran errands. Paul worked from sunrise to sunset. Paul knew it wasn't how fast you worked, but how well you worked.

Paul watched his father work. Much of

this was familiar. All his life, Paul had seen his father shaping silver. Now Paul watched closely to learn to be a silversmith himself.

Paul worked hard to master the silversmith's trade. He memorized the recipe for making strong silver. He mixed the right amount of silver with the right amount of copper. If Paul mixed the wrong amounts, the silver would be too soft to hold its shape or too hard for him to hammer.

Paul heated flat pieces of silver until he could bend them into the shapes he wanted. As the silver cooled, Paul heated it, hammered it, and heated it again. Paul learned how to bend soft silver and trim rough edges. Paul's father taught him how to attach legs onto pots. He showed Paul how to make teapots, coffeepots, spoons, buttons, buckles, spurs, tankards, sugar dishes, tongs, and even shakers for dry mustard. Paul made candlesticks and cups for churches.

Paul kept his tools clean and sharp. He knew dull tools left scratches on silver. Scratches would damage his reputation as an

up-and-coming silversmith. Paul polished silver until it shone like a mirror.

Paul waited on customers. He showed them silver pieces his father had made. Paul carefully wrote new orders in his father's account book. Paul weighed silver, gold, and copper. He accurately wrote those measurements. Paul learned how to draw. If a customer wanted a special teapot, Paul drew the teapot first. Paul engraved flowers, designs, and words on bowls, teapots, and plates.

Paul's father didn't pay him money for his hard work. When Paul was fifteen years old, he formed a bell ringer's club with five friends. They signed a contract to ring the bells at Christ Church for one year. They rang the eight big bells for two hours each week.

The boys climbed over 150 stairs to reach the bells. Paul had to be strong to ring the heavy bells. The largest bell weighed 1,545 pounds and the smallest bell weighed 620 pounds! The bells were rung from below, by pulling on long ropes. Each bell made a different sound. Every bell had these words engraved onto it: *We are the first ring of bells cast for the British Empire in North America.*

Paul enjoyed seeing Boston's many sights. Trained dogs did special tricks. Actors put on plays. Polar bears performed. There was even a pickled pirate's head to stare at!

For a small fee, Paul could see Mr. Fletcher's mechanical toys. There was a mechanical man playing music. Mechanical birds flew in a forest. There was a miniature town with a thousand moving parts. Tiny ships sailed. Small coaches and wagons rolled. A miniature mill ground powder. Paul saw the sun, moon, and planets spinning in their orbits at the moving planetarium.

Mrs. Hiller's waxworks was another unusual Boston sight. Paul saw wax dummies of kings and queens.

Back in his father's shop, Paul worked hard. He wanted to become a master silversmith like his father. Paul knew if he did well he might inherit the Revere shop.

5
Paul Revere, Silversmith and Soldier

That day came sooner than Paul expected. On July 22, 1754, Paul's father died. Paul said his father left his family with "a good name." He also left his silversmith business.

Paul's mother now owned the silver shop. Paul was nineteen and too young to own the shop. He had to be twenty-one to inherit his father's business. Under his mother's guidance, Paul kept the shop open.

Paul's mother paid a silver thimble and money to Dr. Clark to rent their home and shop. Soon, it was Paul's job to pay the rent. Paul's first payment was ten silver rings and cash.

Paul's brother Thomas helped in the silver

shop. Paul trained Thomas to do the silver-smithing jobs he had learned from their father.

Paul had to care for his mother as well as his brothers and sisters. Paul worked long hours to provide food, clothing, and shelter for his family. Then suddenly, despite his responsibilities, Paul joined the army! Britain and France were fighting over land west of Massachusetts. In 1755, one out of every eight men in Massachusetts marched off to fight the French. In 1756, Paul felt it was his turn to serve. He was twenty-one.

At the same time, a young man from Virginia named George Washington joined the army, too. George was two years older than Paul. One day, Paul and George would become famous for their roles in the Revolutionary War.

Paul signed on to fight for one year. He was a second lieutenant. The soldiers in his group marched to Lake George in New York. Paul carried his own gun and hatchet. The militia provided Paul with two spoons, a can-

teen, a knapsack, a blanket, a bullet pouch, and a horn for gunpowder.

Paul marched to Albany, New York. He joined other colonial soldiers as they trooped to Lake George. Paul camped at Fort William Henry. The men cut down trees and built boats. The plan was to cross Lake George and attack the French.

The soldiers built a hundred boats, but they never attacked the French. Too many soldiers were sick from poor food and dirty drinking water. Six to eight men died each day.

Paul's summer was long, hot, and boring. He missed the bustle of Boston. He missed his family and friends. He cut down trees, cleaned his rifle, and fought off the biting black flies that pestered everyone. Sometimes the flies were so noisy that the soldiers couldn't hear their enemies sneaking up on them.

In November, Paul was ordered back to Boston. The armies wouldn't fight in the freezing winter weather. Hungry, tired, and cold, Paul walked home. But there must have been a spring in his step. Paul Revere was going back to Boston!

Paul returned to the silversmith shop. He was twenty-one and the shop belonged to him. His father's tools were now Paul's tools. His father's silver molds were his, too.

Paul set out to make a name for himself as a silversmith. His father had left his "good name" when he died. Paul had to earn his own good name to compete with Boston's other silversmiths. These silversmiths were older and more experienced than Paul.

Paul was confident in his skills. He rolled up his sleeves, tied on his apron, and went to work. Before long, Paul was making over ninety different objects. Most were made out of silver, but Paul used gold, too. Paul made teapots, coffeepots, sugar bowls, spoons, sugar tongs, dishes, buckles, buttons, trays, and thimbles. Paul created handles for pistols and hilts for swords. He shaped silver whistles for children. He created candlesticks, funnels, pipes, and instruments for doctors. He made dog collars, baby rattles, and faces for clocks. Paul made gold thimbles, rings, beads, buttons, and bracelets.

One customer wanted a silver collar for his pet squirrel. Paul made it. His cousin needed a branding iron. Paul made it. Students wanted a special tankard for their teacher. Paul made it. One rich customer wanted a silver dish made from an ostrich egg. Paul made that, too!

Paul proudly stamped his name or initials on the things he made. He put PR on small pieces. He stamped REVERE or P. REVERE on larger pieces. Everyone could see that Paul Revere had done the fine work.

Paul turned his artistic talents to engraving. He engraved pictures into a copper plate with a sharp tool. He printed pictures from the engraved plate and sold them.

Paul engraved songbooks, advertisements, and cartoons for newspapers. He printed pamphlets. Paul signed his pictures: *Engraved, Printed, and Sold by Paul Revere.*

Paul repaired things. No job was too small for Paul Revere. If a cup had a dent, Paul hammered it out. If a teapot's handle was broken, Paul repaired it. If a tea set had a missing spoon, Paul made one to match. If a rider's spurs were snapped, Paul fixed them. He even repaired umbrellas.

Paul was also a dentist. He cleaned teeth. He made false teeth out of hippopotamus tusks! When someone lost a front tooth, Paul made a new one. Paul used silver wire to secure the tooth into the person's mouth.

In a newspaper ad, Paul wrote that he made false teeth that looked "natural." Paul asked his customers to come to "Paul Revere, Goldsmith, near the Head of Dr. Clarke's Wharf, Boston." Paul was so busy that sometimes he hired other silversmiths to help him.

6

Paul Revere, Parent and Patriot

Paul wasn't too busy to marry, however. On August 17, 1757, Paul married twenty-year-old Sara Orne. Paul nicknamed her "Sary." Sary joined Paul, his mother, and his younger brothers and sisters in the crowded Revere home.

In 1758, Paul and Sary had their first child. They named her Deborah, after Paul's mother and grandmother. Their second child was born in 1760. He was named Paul, after his father and grandfather. Sara, who was named after her mother, was born in 1763. Paul and Sary had eight children. Paul lovingly called his children "his lambs."

In 1764, one of Paul and Sary's daughters

had a high fever. She broke out into a rash. The little girl had the dreaded smallpox. Paul was told to take his daughter to a pesthouse. This is where people with smallpox went so that they didn't spread the disease. Most people who went to the pesthouse died. Paul and Sary refused to let their daughter be taken to the deadly pesthouse. They cared for her at home.

Paul hung a flag outside his door to warn people that someone inside had smallpox. Paul let his furnace burn out. He put away his tools, shut his account book, and closed his shop door. A guard outside Paul's door made sure the Reveres stayed inside.

The Reveres were locked in their home for a month. When the little girl recovered, the Reveres once again opened their doors.

Paul hurried to his shop. He hadn't made any money for a month. It was time to get back to work!

Paul had many regular customers who bought things in his shop. John Singleton Copley, an artist, was one of Paul's customers. Mr. Copley was well-known for his beautiful portraits. Paul made silver and gold frames for Mr. Copley's small pictures.

Mr. Copley painted Paul sitting at his workbench. His deep, bold, brown eyes stare out of the picture. Paul is wearing his every-day work clothes. Paul's left hand is under his chin, as if he was thinking hard. He holds a beautifully polished teapot in his left hand.

Paul sat for many long hours while Mr. Copley painted. But it was worth it. Mr. Copley captured the real Paul Revere.

Paul was busy from dawn to dusk. In the evening, Paul enjoyed being with his many friends. Paul also joined several groups to discuss problems with Britain.

Britain and her American colonies weren't getting along. Britain passed laws making the American colonists pay taxes. The American colonists said the taxes were unfair. One law, called the Stamp Act, was passed in February of 1765. The Stamp Act said that American colonists must pay a tax on paper, documents, newspaper, and playing cards.

Paul protested against the Stamp Act. He felt the tax was unfair because American colonists did not get to vote on the tax. Paul and his fellow Patriots joined a group called "the Sons of Liberty." The group often gathered for meetings and protests at a large tree, which became known as the Liberty Tree.

In March of 1766, the Stamp Act ended because American colonists refused to buy British goods. On May 19, 1766, there was a big celebration. Church bells rang. Cannons fired. Drums were beaten. Strolling musicians played flutes and violins. That night, fireworks exploded in the sky.

Men, women, and children carrying lanterns quietly marched through the streets. They gathered at the Liberty Tree. Sailors had hung lanterns from the Liberty Tree's branches. Paul Revere engraved this scene on copper, printed copies, and sold them.

But the difficulties between Britain and America grew worse. Britain announced a new tax on glass, tea, lead, and paint. Paul and the Sons of Liberty protested again.

Many others joined them. Americans stopped buying British things. They stopped drinking British tea. This time, they went one step further. They wrote a letter asking colonists in the other twelve American colonies to join Massachusetts in fighting the taxes.

King George III of Britain was angry when he learned about the letter. He ordered the Massachusetts government to take back the letter. Instead, the Massachusetts government voted ninety-two to seventeen to disobey King George!

Paul Revere made a special silver punch bowl to celebrate. He proudly stamped his name on the bottom of the bowl.

Paul made fun of the seventeen men who voted to take back the letter. He engraved a picture of them marching into a dragon's mouth.

King George wouldn't give up. He sent thousands of British soldiers to Boston. Paul wrote about the soldiers when they arrived on September 30, 1768. He drew a picture of the eight British ships in Boston Harbor.

The British soldiers made things worse. They camped on Boston Common. They were rude. They knocked people into the street. They sang loud songs during church.

"Yankee Doodle" was one of the favorite songs the British soldiers sang to make the Patriots angry. It was an insulting song to Americans. Later, however, "Yankee Doodle" became a favorite song of patriotic Americans. The Americans called out to the red-coated British soldiers "Bloodybacks!" Boys yelled "Lobster for Sale!" when they saw the British soldiers. Soldiers were bumped off bridges and wharves.

The Americans and the British knew some small spark could set off a huge explosion.

7
Paul Revere, Patriot Artist

That spark came on March 5, 1770. A foot of snow fell and the streets were slippery. British soldiers pushed Americans into the icy streets. Boston boys boasted they were going to clean out the Bloodybacks.

A crowd gathered at a building where some British soldiers lived. A British soldier guarded the building. The crowd threw snowballs, oyster shells, and chunks of ice at the British soldier. They called him names. The British soldier ran out of patience. When a boy shouted something at the British soldier, the soldier hit him in the head with his gun. The boy wasn't even knocked down. The crowd threatened the soldier.

Suddenly, the bells in a nearby church began clanging the warning for "Fire!" People, thinking it was a fire, rushed to the scene.

The British soldier yelled for help. Captain Preston, the officer in command of the British soldiers in the area, took seven soldiers and ran to the British soldier's aid. The captain ordered his men to raise their rifles. But he didn't order them to fire into the crowd. Someone, however, did shout, "Fire!"

The crowd moved closer to the soldiers. *Bang! Bang!* One by one, the British soldiers shot into the crowd. Men and boys fell, wounded and dying.

More British soldiers rushed to rescue their friends. It was a standoff between the American colonists and the British soldiers.

Thomas Hutchinson, the lieutenant governor of Massachusetts, spoke to both sides. He promised that justice would be done.

Captain Preston and his men were arrested. The angry people of Boston buried the five men who had died. They called the fight "the Boston Massacre."

Paul Revere made an engraving of the

Boston Massacre. He printed pictures from this engraving. The pictures were hand-colored with bright colors. Paul wanted people to see the red of the British uniforms and the red of the colonists' blood.

Paul's picture wasn't accurate. He left out the snow. He made the sky blue even though the fight took place at night. Paul drew Captain Preston raising his sword. Paul engraved the soldiers all firing at the same time when they really fired one at a time. Paul drew seven men dying, but only five died. Paul didn't want his picture to show exactly what happened. He wanted it to make people angry. He wanted them to remember that British soldiers had shot and killed colonists.

Paul's picture was very popular. People hung it in special places in their homes. It was taken to the other colonies. American Patriots everywhere were angry about the massacre.

The picture was taken to Britain. People there grew angry, too. Many people in Britain didn't want the British soldiers shooting

American colonists. An uneasy truce settled over Boston.

Paul returned to his job as a silversmith. He also bought his first home. The Reveres' new home was a wooden house on North Square. It was a block away from the busy Boston wharves. Paul's new neighbors included another silversmith, two tailors, a boatbuilder, merchants, ministers, and families. Paul's Hitchbourn cousins lived nearby.

The Revere house was two stories tall with an attic. The Reveres walked through their backyard to Cockerel Church. The "new" Revere house was ninety years old in 1770. Today, Paul Revere's house is the oldest home still standing in downtown Boston.

A water well and market were across the cobblestone street in North Square. Paul sometimes served as the market clerk. He made sure the market opened and closed at the right time. He watched to see that no one was cheated.

In May of 1773, Paul's wife, Sary, died. Paul had to care for his eight children alone.

Later that year, Paul married Rachel Walker. Paul wrote Rachel a special love poem in which he spelled out R-A-C-H-E-L. Paul and Rachel had eight children together. Paul Revere's home was a crowded, noisy, lively place.

Paul was very busy with his family, church, and business. But Paul still found time to learn more about the British laws that upset so many colonists. Paul joined friends to talk about British laws. He met with the Sons of Liberty to discuss what they could do about the tax that still remained on tea. The American colonists decided not to pay the tea tax. They told the British not to ship any more tea to America.

On November 28, 1773, however, a ship named the *Dartmouth* sailed into Boston. The ship docked at Griffith's Wharf. On November 29, Paul and twenty-five companions guarded the *Dartmouth* to make sure that the tea was not unloaded.

8

Paul Revere Joins the Boston Tea Party

Two more tea ships docked alongside the *Dartmouth* at Griffith's Wharf. They were the *Beaver* and the *Eleanor*. Three hundred forty-two chests of tea were on the three ships.

The Sons of Liberty were determined not to let one leaf of tea be unloaded. On December 16, 1773, seven thousand people gathered to hear speeches about the tea. Paul Revere was one of them.

Sam Adams, a Patriot leader, said, "This meeting can do nothing more to save the country." This was a signal for 150 selected Patriots to dress as Mohawk Indians. They were to go to Griffith's Wharf.

"Boston Harbor a teapot tonight!" a Patriot shouted.

Quickly and quietly, the Patriots opened each tea chest. They dumped the tea into the sea. The Patriots were careful not to damage anything but the tea. Anyone who tried to steal tea was punished.

Paul was sent on another mission. He was to ride to New York and Philadelphia to spread the news about the Boston Tea Party.

Paul rode hard and fast. In eleven days, he rode eight hundred miles over rough roads and trails. Patriots everywhere were pleased to hear the news about the tea party.

Paul returned to Boston on December 27. He must have smiled when he heard people singing about "Bold Revere" and the Boston Tea Party. The Boston Tea Party made many American Patriots happy. But it made King George very angry. The king decided to punish Boston. He ordered Boston to pay for the tea. He sent more soldiers to Boston to live in people's homes. The soldiers would guard

Boston Neck, the narrow strip of land connecting Boston to the mainland, to make sure Patriots outside of Boston had difficulty communicating with people in Boston.

King George said only his warships could sail into or out of Boston. No other ships would be allowed into Boston Harbor. This hurt the colonists. Ships were very important to Boston. Without the ships, food, clothing, and other supplies were hard to get. Sea captains, sailors, merchants, sailmakers, boatbuilders, rope makers, and fishermen lost their jobs. Paul lost business because no one could afford silver. But the people of Boston wouldn't pay a penny for the tea.

Patriots in the other colonies helped Boston. They sent wagons full of food and firewood into Boston over Boston Neck. Herds of cattle also passed over the Neck and into Boston. Life was difficult, but the Patriots wouldn't give in to the British.

In 1775, Paul closed his silver shop. He decided to spend his time fighting against the British. Paul didn't shoot at them. Instead, he spied on them. Paul slipped out of Boston to carry messages to the other colonies. He did whatever he could against the British.

In the spring of 1775, the British learned that Patriots in the towns around Boston were gathering guns, bullets, cannons, and gunpowder. They would use these weapons if the British dared to march out of Boston to attack the American colonists.

Patriots also trained to fight. Some of these men were ready to leave their farms and families in a minute to go to war. They called themselves "Minutemen."

In April of 1775, Paul knew the British were making plans. They wanted to capture the Patriots' guns and gunpowder in Concord, Massachusetts. Sam Adams and John Hancock, two Patriot leaders, were staying in Lexington, on the road to Concord. The British hoped to capture the Patriot leaders and the weapons in one swift attack.

9
Paul Revere's Midnight Ride

No Patriot knew exactly when the British were going to leave Boston. They didn't know if the British would march out through the guarded gate at Boston Neck or if they would row across the Charles River and march from Charlestown. Paul decided to make a signal to warn the Patriots when the British were coming. One lighted lantern in the tall tower of Christ Church meant the British were marching over Boston Neck. Two shining lanterns meant the British were crossing the Charles River.

Paul knew the tower of Christ Church very well. He had spent hours in the tower ringing the heavy bells. Paul knew the lights could be seen in Charlestown.

On April 18, 1775, Paul learned that the British were marching out that night! He sent Robert Newman, his friend and fellow Patriot, to the church tower. Robert knew the signal: "One if by land, two if by sea." Robert lit two lanterns.

A full moon hung in the sky. Two men rowed Paul very quietly across the river. They had to sneak under the cannons of the *Somerset*, a British warship.

Patriots were waiting for Paul when he reached the opposite shore. They had seen the two lanterns. Paul put on his spurs, jumped on a borrowed horse, and galloped away on his midnight ride.

"The Regulars are coming! The Regulars are coming!" Paul shouted as he rode. A "Regular" was a British soldier. Paul tried not to make too much noise. He wanted to avoid British patrols.

Other riders took Paul's message to the farms and villages scattered around the countryside. Minutemen quickly prepared to fight. Paul stopped in Lexington. He warned

Sam Adams and John Hancock that the British soldiers were coming to get them. Billy Dawes was another Patriot messenger. As Paul was crossing the Charles River, Billy had crossed Boston Neck to carry the same warning about the marching British. Billy joined Paul in Lexington. Paul and Billy rode toward Concord, which was a few miles away. They were joined by Dr. Samuel Prescott, another Patriot.

The British knew Paul and other riders were out. Before Paul, Billy, and Dr. Prescott could reach Concord, they ran into a British patrol. Dr. Prescott smacked his horse, jumped a stone wall, and galloped away. Billy Dawes escaped in the opposite direction.

Six soldiers chased Paul. They stopped his horse. They aimed their pistols at Paul. Paul surrendered.

The British were pleased to have captured bold Paul Revere. They threatened to shoot Paul if he didn't tell them what he was doing.

Suddenly, Paul and the soldiers heard a shot in the distance. Paul said that was the

signal to alert the Minutemen. The British soldiers decided to leave. They took Paul's horse. They left Paul standing on the road as they galloped off.

Paul Revere's midnight ride was over, but he still had more work to do. He walked back to Lexington to make sure Sam Adams and John Hancock had escaped.

Paul was surprised to find the two Patriots still in Lexington. Paul told them to hurry. Finally, Adams and Hancock got into a carriage. Paul guided them out of town. When Paul was sure they were safe, he returned to Lexington.

At dawn, Paul saw hundreds of British soldiers marching into Lexington. Seventy-five Minutemen faced the British on Lexington Green. Paul and another man grabbed the heavy trunk and carried it toward a nearby forest.

Paul heard a rifle shot. He turned around to look, but a building blocked his view. Paul couldn't see whether the Patriots or the British had fired first. Paul heard more shots.

Smoke swirled over Lexington Green. When the smoke cleared, eight Patriots lay dead. The Revolutionary War had begun.

The British marched to Concord. Paul couldn't ride ahead to warn the Concord Minutemen. Fortunately, Dr. Prescott had reached Concord. Hundreds of Minutemen gathered to face the British.

A battle began at Concord's North Bridge. The Patriots forced the British to retreat into town. When they saw more Minutemen gathering to fight them, the British decided to retreat to Boston.

As the British retreated, the Minutemen fired at them. The Minutemen shot from behind fences, walls, and trees. Many British soldiers were killed or wounded. By nightfall, the tired, defeated, angry British returned to the safety of Boston.

Paul Revere's courageous ride had given the Patriots the warning they needed to beat the British.

Paul Revere & Son,

10
Paul Revere
Becomes Famous

Paul Revere's famous ride was at the beginning of the Revolutionary War. The war lasted from 1775 until 1783. When the war ended, the thirteen American colonies had become the thirteen United States. They were no longer ruled by Britain.

After his ride, Paul couldn't return to Boston. He lived outside of town with his family until the British left Boston in 1776. When he returned to Boston, Paul went back to his shop. But he did very little silversmithing because of the war. Not many people could afford silver.

During the remainder of the war, Paul

used his many talents to help the United States win the Revolutionary War. He made more rides to spread news, carry messages, and give warnings. Paul did engraving, too. He engraved and printed paper money for the State of Massachusetts. He learned how to make gunpowder.

Paul became a lieutenant colonel in the Massachusetts artillery. He commanded the fort on Castle Island. Paul kept his men and their cannons ready in case the British attacked Boston.

In March of 1779, Paul recovered twenty-one cannons from a British ship wrecked on a beach. It was the *Somerset*, the same ship Paul had slipped past on the night of his midnight ride. The United States desperately needed the *Somerset*'s cannons. Paul took the cannons to protect Boston.

That summer, Paul left Boston to attack a new British fort in Maine. He was in charge of seven cannons. The attack was a disaster. Over five hundred Americans were captured. Paul's cannons were captured, too, but he escaped. He walked many miles home to Boston.

Paul was blamed for his role in the defeat. Later, however, Paul was cleared of the charges against him.

In 1779, Paul reopened his silver shop. He needed money to care for the twelve members of his family living at home.

On April 19, 1783, the Revolutionary War finally ended. This was almost eight years after Paul had made his midnight ride.

Paul turned many of his jobs in the silver shop over to his son Paul. After the war, more people could afford silver again. Cheap tea was available and his son sold many tea sets. The account books showed that he sold four times as much silver as he had before the war.

Paul opened a hardware store. He sold items made of brass, copper, iron, and pewter. He also sold china, knives, forks, goblets, and mirrors.

By 1786, Paul moved his hardware shop to the center of Boston. When Paul stood on the steps of his store, he could see the new Massachusetts State House as well as the site of the Boston Massacre.

Many hardware items that Paul sold had been made in England. Paul decided to make his own things to sell. He designed and built an iron factory. Paul made nails, spikes, and bolts for the many ships being built in Boston.

In 1792, the old bell at Cockerel Church cracked. Paul offered to melt the old bell and cast a new one. This was something Paul had never done before. But he believed that he could do the job well.

Paul learned about bell making. Then he rolled up his sleeves and went to work. He melted down the old bell, added new metal, and cast a one-thousand-pound bell. Paul carefully engraved on the rim of the bell *The first bell cast in Boston 1792 P. Revere.* Paul's son Joseph joined him at his factory. Together they cast more than three hundred bells. They also made cannons.

Then Paul turned his attention to copper.

Most copper had to be shipped from England. Paul decided to make his own. He was soon making brass and copper materials for ships.

Paul put his mind to discovering how to roll copper into large, flat sheets. Until then, such sheets had to be bought from England. Paul made copper sheets for the towering new dome of the Massachusetts State House. Paul made flat sheets of copper for ships. The copper was put on the bottoms of ships to keep out shipworms, which ate holes in the wooden ships.

Paul supplied many things for the new ship the *Constitution*. Paul made nails, bolts, and spikes. Paul made copper for the *Constitution*'s bottom after the first layer of copper wore out. He even made the *Constitution*'s bell. Today, the *Constitution* is the oldest ship in the United States Navy. It is nicknamed *Old Ironsides* because cannonballs bounced off it. *Old Ironsides* is the most famous ship in America.

Over the years, Paul made fewer and fewer silver pieces. In 1811, he retired from business. He was seventy-seven years old. Paul and Rachel wanted to spend their remaining years enjoying their many grandchildren.

Rachel Revere died in 1813. Paul lived for five more years. He died on May 10, 1818. He was eighty-three years old. When Paul Revere died, a Revere bell rang eighty-three times in his honor.

Paul Revere was buried in the Old Granary Burying Ground in Boston. Many of Paul's family members were buried there, too. Sam Adams, John Hancock, and other Patriots are also buried at Old Granary.

On April 18, 1775, Paul Revere began his famous midnight ride to warn Adams, Hancock, and the Minutemen that the British were coming. For many years, few people remembered Paul Revere's midnight ride. When Henry Wadsworth Longfellow published "Paul Revere's Ride" in 1861, however, Paul Revere became famous.

Who would have guessed what an important silversmith, businessman, parent, Patriot, and messenger Paul Revere would become when he was born that chilly December day in 1734?